BIBLE
PROMISES
TO LIVE BY

**New Living
Translation.**
SECOND EDITION

 Tyndale House Publishers, Inc. Carol Stream, Illinois

TYNDALE and Tyndale's quill logo are registered trademarks of Tyndale House Publishers, Inc.

Bible Promises to Live By

Copyright © 2007 by Ron Beers. All rights reserved.

Designed by Jennifer Ghionzoli

Scripture quotations are taken from the *Holy Bible,* New Living Translation, copyright © 1996, 2004. Used by permission of Tyndale House Publishers, Inc., Carol Stream, Illinois 60188. All rights reserved.

ISBN-13: 978-1-4143-1355-9
ISBN-10: 1-4143-1355-1

Printed in the United Kingdom

13 12 11 10 09 08
 8   7   6   5   4   3

CONTENTS

——— ༄ ———

BIBLE PROMISES TO LIVE BY

——— ༄༅ ———

INTRODUCTION

—— ✺ ——

When people make promises, do you ever doubt they will follow through? Has anyone you've trusted broken a promise to you? Have you ever made a promise you couldn't keep, or didn't intend to keep? Thankfully, God keeps all his promises. This makes his Word, the Bible, the greatest of treasures because it is filled with promises that you know will be kept. These are promises God makes not only to his people in general but to you personally. One of God's greatest promises is that his Word will last forever (Isaiah 40:8; Matthew 24:35; 1 Peter 1:23-25), which means his promises will also stand for eternity. Because of this, we can trust that all God's promises will come true. This is the bedrock of our faith, what gives us hope, encouragement, and comfort. Whereas human promises often fail and disappoint us, God's promises fulfill and sustain us by providing guidance, teaching, encouragement, forgiveness, joy, and the confidence that our future is secure.

This little book introduces you to many of God's promises—more than 750 promises from God covering seventy different topics. It covers some of

God's greatest and most personal promises. The topics selected in this book cover different times and walks of life to show that God's care and concern extend to all people for all time, including you! God's promises are as ancient as they are current and fresh, which means they apply as much to your past and present as they do to your future. His promises are relevant in your most needy hour, as well as in your times of blessing and in the routine of everyday life. Knowing God's promises will help you discover what God desires for your life and how to receive and enjoy all that God has in store for you.

ANGER

Yahweh! The LORD! The God of compassion and mercy! I am slow to anger and filled with unfailing love and faithfulness.

Exodus 34:6

You are a God of forgiveness, gracious and merciful, slow to become angry, and rich in unfailing love.

Nehemiah 9:17

His anger lasts only a moment, but his favor lasts a lifetime! Weeping may last through the night, but joy comes with the morning.

Psalm 30:5

Stop being angry! Turn from your rage! Do not lose your temper— it only leads to harm.

Psalm 37:8

The LORD is compassionate and merciful, slow to get angry and filled with unfailing love

Psalm 103:8

A gentle answer deflects anger, but harsh words make tempers flare.

Proverbs 15:1

Sensible people control their temper; they earn respect by over-looking wrongs.

Proverbs 19:11

If you are even angry with someone, you are subject to judgment!

Matthew 5:22

Dear friends, never take revenge. Leave that to the righteous anger of God. For the Scriptures say, "I will take revenge; I will pay them back," says the LORD.

Romans 12:19

"Don't sin by letting anger control you." Don't let the sun go down while you are still angry, for anger gives a foothold to the devil.

Ephesians 4:26-27

Get rid of all bitterness, rage, anger, harsh words, and slander, as well as all types of evil behavior. Instead, be kind to each other, tenderhearted, forgiving one another, just as God through Christ has forgiven you.

Ephesians 4:31-32

Understand this, my dear brothers and sisters: You must all be quick to listen, slow to speak, and slow to get angry. Human anger does not produce the righteousness God desires.

James 1:19-20

He did not retaliate when he was insulted, nor threaten revenge when he suffered. He left his case in the hands of God, who always judges fairly.

1 Peter 2:23

ANXIETY

—— ‿◯‿ ——

Commit everything you do to the LORD. Trust him, and he will help you.

Psalm 37:5

God is our refuge and strength, always ready to help in times of trouble. So we will not fear when earthquakes come and the mountains crumble into the sea. Let the oceans roar and foam. Let the mountains tremble as the waters surge!

Psalm 46:1-3

Give your burdens to the LORD, and he will take care of you.

Psalm 55:22

Teach us to realize the brevity of life, so that we may grow in wisdom.

Psalm 90:12

The LORD helps the fallen and lifts those bent beneath their loads.

Psalm 145:14

This righteousness will bring peace. Yes, it will bring quietness and confidence forever.

Isaiah 32:17

Blessed are those who trust in the LORD and have made the LORD their hope and confidence. They are like trees planted along a riverbank, with roots that reach deep into the water. Such trees are not bothered by the heat or worried by long months of drought. Their leaves stay green, and they never stop producing fruit.

Jeremiah 17:7-8

Can all your worries add a single moment to your life?

Matthew 6:27

Don't worry about these things, saying, "What will we eat? What will we drink? What will we wear?" These things dominate the thoughts of unbelievers, but your heavenly Father already knows all your needs.

Matthew 6:31-32

We know that God causes everything to work together for the good of those who love God and are called according to his purpose for them.

Romans 8:28

Don't worry about anything; instead, pray about everything. Tell God what you need, and thank him for all he has done. Then you will experience God's peace, which exceeds anything we can understand. His peace will guard your hearts and minds as you live in Christ Jesus.

Philippians 4:6-7

This same God who takes care of me will supply all your needs from his glorious riches, which have been given to us in Christ Jesus.

Philippians 4:19

Give all your worries and cares to God, for he cares about you.

1 Peter 5:7

BELIEF

"What do you mean, 'If I can'?" Jesus asked. "Anything is possible if a person believes."

Mark 9:23

To all who believed him and accepted him, he gave the right to become children of God.

John 1:12

God loved the world so much that he gave his one and only Son, so that everyone who believes in him will not perish but have eternal life.

John 3:16

Anyone who believes in God's Son has eternal life.

John 3:36

Jesus replied, "I am the bread of life. Whoever comes to me will never be hungry again. Whoever believes in me will never be thirsty."

John 6:35

I tell you the truth, anyone who believes has eternal life.

John 6:47

Jesus told him, "You believe because you have seen me. Blessed are those who believe without seeing me."

John 20:29

He is the one all the prophets testified about, saying that everyone who believes in him will have their sins forgiven through his name.

Acts 10:43

BLESSINGS

May it please you to bless the house of your servant, so that it may continue forever before you. For you have spoken, and when you grant a blessing to your servant, O Sovereign LORD, it is an eternal blessing!

2 Samuel 7:29

How great is the goodness you have stored up for those who fear you. You lavish it on those who come to you for protection, blessing them before the watching world.

Psalm 31:19

The LORD will withhold no good thing from those who do what is right.

Psalm 84:11

Blessed are those who trust in the LORD and have made the LORD their hope and confidence.

Jeremiah 17:7

Let's not get tired of doing what is good. At just the right time we will reap a harvest of blessing if we don't give up.

Galatians 6:9

All who are victorious will inherit all these blessings.

Revelation 21:7

COMFORT

Even when I walk through the darkest valley, I will not be afraid, for you are close beside me. Your rod and your staff protect and comfort me.

Psalm 23:4

His anger lasts only a moment, but his favor lasts a lifetime! Weeping may last through the night, but joy comes with the morning.

Psalm 30:5

Give your burdens to the LORD, and he will take care of you. He will not permit the godly to slip and fall.

Psalm 55:22

You keep track of all my sorrows. You have collected all my tears in your bottle. You have recorded each one in your book.

Psalm 56:8

Remember your promise to me; it is my only hope. Your promise revives me; it comforts me in all my troubles.

Psalm 119:49-50

I meditate on your age-old regulations; O LORD, they comfort me.

Psalm 119:52

The LORD himself watches over you! The LORD stands beside you as your protective shade. The sun will not harm you by day, nor the moon at night.

Psalm 121:5-6

The LORD helps the fallen and lifts those bent beneath their loads.

Psalm 145:14

He heals the brokenhearted and bandages their wounds.

Psalm 147:3

In all their suffering he also suffered, and he personally rescued them. In his love and mercy he redeemed them. He lifted them up and carried them through all the years.

Isaiah 63:9

God blesses those who mourn, for they will be comforted.

Matthew 5:4

Then Jesus said, "Come to me, all of you who are weary and carry heavy burdens, and I will give you rest."

Matthew 11:28

What is the price of five sparrows—two copper coins? Yet God does not forget a single one of them. And the very hairs on your head are all numbered. So don't be afraid; you are more valuable to God than a whole flock of sparrows.

Luke 12:6-7

I have told you all this so that you may have peace in me. Here on earth you will have many trials and sorrows. But take heart, because I have overcome the world.

John 16:33

God is our merciful Father and the source of all comfort. He comforts us in all our troubles so that we can comfort others. When they are troubled, we will be able to give them the same comfort God has given us.

2 Corinthians 1:3-4

The more we suffer for Christ, the more God will shower us with his comfort through Christ.

2 Corinthians 1:5

The Lamb on the throne will be their Shepherd. He will lead them to springs of life-giving water. And God will wipe every tear from their eyes.

Revelation 7:17

CONTENTMENT

He satisfies the thirsty and fills the hungry with good things.

Psalm 107:9

Don't envy sinners, but always continue to fear the LORD. You will be rewarded for this; your hope will not be disappointed.

Proverbs 23:17-18

Not that I was ever in need, for I have learned how to be content with whatever I have. I know how to live on almost nothing or with everything. I have learned the secret of living in every situation, whether it is with a full stomach or empty, with plenty or little. For I can do everything through Christ, who gives me strength.

Philippians 4:11-13

Don't love money; be satisfied with what you have. For God has said, "I will never fail you. I will never abandon you."

Hebrews 13:5

By his divine power, God has given us everything we need for living a godly life. We have received all of this by coming to know him, the one who called us to himself by means of his marvelous glory and excellence.

2 Peter 1:3

COURAGE

Be strong and courageous! Do not be afraid and do not panic before them. For the LORD your God will personally go ahead of you. He will neither fail you nor abandon you.

Deuteronomy 31:6

This is my command—be strong and courageous! Do not be afraid or discouraged. For the LORD your God is with you wherever you go.

Joshua 1:9

Who is God except the LORD? Who but our God is a solid rock? God arms me with strength, and he makes my way perfect.

Psalm 18:31-32

The LORD is my light and my salvation—so why should I be afraid? The LORD is my fortress, protecting me from danger, so why should I tremble?

Psalm 27:1

The LORD is my strength and shield. I trust him with all my heart. He helps me, and my heart is filled with joy.

Psalm 28:7

Don't be afraid, for I am with you. Don't be discouraged, for I am your God. I will strengthen you and help you. I will hold you up with my victorious right hand.

Isaiah 41:10

O Israel, the one who formed you says, "Do not be afraid, for I have ransomed you. I have called you by name; you are mine."

Isaiah 43:1

When you are brought to trial in the synagogues and before rulers and authorities, don't worry about how to defend yourself or what to say, for the Holy Spirit will teach you at that time what needs to be said.

Luke 12:11-12

If the old way, which has been replaced, was glorious, how much more glorious is the new, which remains forever! Since this new way gives us such confidence, we can be very bold.

2 Corinthians 3:11-12

I can do everything through Christ, who gives me strength.

Philippians 4:13

DEATH

Even when I walk through the darkest valley, I will not be afraid, for you are close beside me. Your rod and your staff protect and comfort me.

Psalm 23:4

That is what God is like. He is our God forever and ever, and he will guide us until we die.

Psalm 48:14

As for me, God will redeem my life. He will snatch me from the power of the grave.

Psalm 49:15

Don't be afraid of those who want to kill your body; they cannot touch your soul.

Matthew 10:28

God loved the world so much that he gave his one and only Son, so that everyone who believes in him will not perish but have eternal life.

John 3:16

I tell you the truth, anyone who obeys my teaching will never die!

John 8:51

I am the resurrection and the life. Anyone who believes in me will live, even after dying.

John 11:25

The wages of sin is death, but the free gift of God is eternal life through Christ Jesus our Lord.

Romans 6:23

Christ lives within you, so even though your body will die because of sin, the Spirit gives you life because you have been made right with God.

Romans 8:10

I am convinced that nothing can ever separate us from God's love. Neither death nor life, neither angels nor demons, neither our fears for today nor our worries about tomorrow—not even the powers of hell can separate us from God's love. No power in the sky above or in the earth below—indeed, nothing in all creation will ever be able to separate us from the love of God that is revealed in Christ Jesus our Lord.

Romans 8:38-39

That is why we never give up. Though our bodies are dying, our spirits are being renewed every day.

2 Corinthians 4:16

Blessed are those who die in the Lord from now on. Yes, says the Spirit, they are blessed indeed, for they will rest from their hard work; for their good deeds follow them!

Revelation 14:13

DESIRES

Take delight in the LORD, and he will give you your heart's desires. Commit everything you do to the LORD. Trust him, and he will help you.

Psalm 37:4-5

I will give you a new heart, and I will put a new spirit in you. I will take out your stony, stubborn heart and give you a tender, responsive heart.

Ezekiel 36:26

You also should consider yourselves to be dead to the power of sin and alive to God through Christ Jesus. Do not let sin control the way you live; do not give in to sinful desires. . . . Sin is no longer your master, for you no longer live under the requirements of the law. Instead, you live under the freedom of God's grace.

Romans 6:11-14

Don't you realize that your body is the temple of the Holy Spirit, who lives in you and was given to you by God? You do not belong to yourself, for God bought you with a high price. So you must honor God with your body.

1 Corinthians 6:19-20

Let the Holy Spirit guide your lives. Then you won't be doing what your sinful nature craves. The sinful nature wants to do evil, which is just the opposite of what the Spirit wants. And the Spirit gives us desires that are the opposite of what the sinful nature desires. These two forces are constantly fighting each other, so you are not free to carry out your good intentions.

Galatians 5:16-17

Those who belong to Christ Jesus have nailed the passions and desires of their sinful nature to his cross and crucified them there.

Galatians 5:24

All of us used to live that way, following the passionate desires and inclinations of our sinful nature. By our very nature we were subject to God's anger, just like everyone else. But God is so rich in mercy, and he loved us so much, that even though we were dead because of our sins, he gave us life when he raised Christ from the dead.

Ephesians 2:3-5

Fix your thoughts on what is true, and honorable, and right, and pure, and lovely, and admirable. Think about things that are excellent and worthy of praise. Keep putting into practice all you learned and received from me—everything you heard from me and saw me doing. Then the God of peace will be with you.

Philippians 4:8-9

Once we, too, were foolish and disobedient. We were misled and became slaves to many lusts and pleasures. Our lives were full of evil and envy, and we hated each other. But—"When God our Savior revealed his kindness and love, he saved us, not because of the righteous things we had done, but because of his mercy. He washed away our sins, giving us a new birth and new life through the Holy Spirit."

Titus 3:3-5

Temptation comes from our own desires, which entice us and drag us away. These desires give birth to sinful actions. And when sin is allowed to grow, it gives birth to death.

James 1:14-15

Because of his glory and excellence, he has given us great and precious promises. These are the promises that enable you to share his divine nature and escape the world's corruption caused by human desires.

2 Peter 1:4

The world offers only a craving for physical pleasure, a craving for everything we see, and pride in our achievements and posses- sions. These are not from the Father, but are from this world. And this world is fading away, along with everything that people crave. But anyone who does what pleases God will live forever.

1 John 2:16-17

DISCIPLINE

Just as a parent disciplines a child, the LORD your God disciplines you for your own good.

Deuteronomy 8:5

Consider the joy of those corrected by God! Do not despise the discipline of the Almighty when you sin. For though he wounds, he also bandages. He strikes, but his hands also heal.

Job 5:17-18

Joyful are those you discipline, LORD, those you teach with your instructions.

Psalm 94:12

The LORD corrects those he loves, just as a father corrects a child in whom he delights.

Proverbs 3:12

The LORD disciplines those he loves, and he punishes each one he accepts as his child.

Hebrews 12:6

Our earthly fathers disciplined us for a few years, doing the best they knew how. But God's discipline is always good for us, so that we might share in his holiness. No discipline is enjoyable while it is happening—it's painful! But afterward there will be a peaceful harvest of right living for those who are trained in this way.

Hebrews 12:10-11

DISCOURAGEMENT

This is my command—be strong and courageous! Do not be afraid or discouraged. For the LORD your God is with you wherever you go.

Joshua 1:9

The LORD is close to the brokenhearted; he rescues those whose spirits are crushed.

Psalm 34:18

He lifted me out of the pit of despair.

Psalm 40:2

Why am I discouraged? Why is my heart so sad? I will put my hope in God! I will praise him again—my Savior and my God!

Psalm 42:5-6

As soon as I pray, you answer me; you encourage me by giving me strength.

Psalm 138:3

Jesus said, "Come to me, all of you who are weary and carry heavy burdens, and I will give you rest."

Matthew 11:28

God blesses you who are hungry now, for you will be satisfied. God blesses you who weep now, for in due time you will laugh.

Luke 6:21

The Scriptures give us hope and encouragement as we wait patiently for God's promises to be fulfilled.

Romans 15:4

The more we suffer for Christ, the more God will shower us with his comfort through Christ.

2 Corinthians 1:5

Each time he said, "My grace is all you need. My power works best in weakness."

2 Corinthians 12:9

Let's not get tired of doing what is good. At just the right time we will reap a harvest of blessing if we don't give up.

Galatians 6:9

May our Lord Jesus Christ himself and God our Father, who loved us and by his grace gave us eternal comfort and a wonderful hope, comfort you and strengthen you in every good thing you do and say.

2 Thessalonians 2:16-17

In his kindness God called you to share in his eternal glory by means of Christ Jesus. So after you have suffered a little while, he will restore, support, and strengthen you, and he will place you on a firm foundation.

1 Peter 5:10

ENEMIES

The LORD your God is going with you! He will fight for you against your enemies, and he will give you victory!

Deuteronomy 20:4

The LORD your God fights for you, just as he has promised.

Joshua 23:10

Victory comes from you, O LORD.

Psalm 3:8

With God's help we will do mighty things, for he will trample down our foes.

Psalm 60:12

You who love the LORD, hate evil! He protects the lives of his godly people and rescues them from the power of the wicked.

Psalm 97:10

Yes, the LORD is for me; he will help me. I will look in triumph at those who hate me.

Psalm 118:7

In that coming day no weapon turned against you will succeed.

Isaiah 54:17

I will rescue you from those you fear so much. Because you trusted me, I will give you your life as a reward. I will rescue you and keep you safe. I, the LORD, have spoken!

Jeremiah 39:17-18

Don't be afraid of those who want to kill your body; they cannot touch your soul.

Matthew 10:28

We have been rescued from our enemies so we can serve God without fear.

Luke 1:74

This includes you who were once far away from God. You were his enemies, separated from him by your evil thoughts and actions. Yet now he has reconciled you to himself through the death of Christ in his physical body. As a result, he has brought you into his own presence, and you are holy and blameless as you stand before him without a single fault.

Colossians 1:21-22

The Lord is faithful; he will strengthen you and guard you from the evil one.

2 Thessalonians 3:3

We can say with confidence, "The LORD is my helper, so I will have no fear. What can mere people do to me?"

Hebrews 13:6

ETERNAL LIFE

After my body has decayed, yet in my body I will see God! I will see him for myself. Yes, I will see him with my own eyes.

Job 19:26-27

Those who die in the LORD will live; their bodies will rise again! Those who sleep in the earth will rise up and sing for joy! For your life-giving light will fall like dew on your people in the place of the dead!

Isaiah 26:19

If you try to hang on to your life, you will lose it. But if you give up your life for my sake, you will save it.

Matthew 16:25

God loved the world so much that he gave his one and only Son, so that everyone who believes in him will not perish but have eternal life.

John 3:16

I tell you the truth, anyone who believes has eternal life.

John 6:47

My sheep listen to my voice; I know them, and they follow me. I give them eternal life, and they will never perish. No one can snatch them away from me.

John 10:27-28

I am the resurrection and the life. Anyone who believes in me will live, even after dying. Everyone who lives in me and believes in me will never ever die.

John 11:25-26

There is more than enough room in my Father's home. If this were not so, would I have told you that I am going to prepare a place for you? When everything is ready, I will come and get you, so that you will always be with me where I am.

John 14:2-3

The wages of sin is death, but the free gift of God is eternal life through Christ Jesus our Lord.

Romans 6:23

Our earthly bodies are planted in the ground when we die, but they will be raised to live forever. Our bodies are buried in brokenness, but they will be raised in glory. They are buried in weakness, but they will be raised in strength.

1 Corinthians 15:42-43

We know that when this earthly tent we live in is taken down (that is, when we die and leave this earthly body), we will have a house in heaven, an eternal body made for us by God himself and not by human hands.

2 Corinthians 5:1

Those who live only to satisfy their own sinful nature will harvest decay and death from that sinful nature. But those who live to please the Spirit will harvest everlasting life from the Spirit.

Galatians 6:8

Anyone who does what pleases God will live forever.

1 John 2:17

You must remain faithful to what you have been taught from the beginning. If you do, you will remain in fellowship with the Son and with the Father. And in this fellowship we enjoy the eternal life he promised us.

1 John 2:24-25

This is what God has testified: He has given us eternal life, and this life is in his Son.

1 John 5:11

I have written this to you who believe in the name of the Son of God, so that you may know you have eternal life.

1 John 5:13

The Lamb on the throne will be their Shepherd. He will lead them to springs of life-giving water. And God will wipe every tear from their eyes.

Revelation 7:17

FAILURE

——— ❧ ❧ ———

The LORD directs the steps of the godly. He delights in every detail of their lives. Though they stumble, they will never fall, for the LORD holds them by the hand.

Psalm 37:23-24

My health may fail, and my spirit may grow weak, but God remains the strength of my heart; he is mine forever.

Psalm 73:26

I still dare to hope when I remember this: The faithful love of the LORD never ends! His mercies never cease.

Lamentations 3:21-22

We know that God causes everything to work together for the good of those who love God and are called according to his purpose for them.

Romans 8:28

Let's not get tired of doing what is good. At just the right time we will reap a harvest of blessing if we don't give up.

Galatians 6:9

I press on to possess that perfection for which Christ Jesus first possessed me. No, dear brothers and sisters, I have not achieved it, but I focus on this one thing: Forgetting the past and looking forward to what lies ahead, I press on to reach the end of the race and receive the heavenly prize for which God, through Christ Jesus, is calling us.

Philippians 3:12-14

God has not given us a spirit of fear and timidity, but of power, love, and self-discipline.

2 Timothy 1:7

Do not throw away this confident trust in the Lord. Remember the great reward it brings you! Patient endurance is what you need now, so that you will continue to do God's will. Then you will receive all that he has promised.

Hebrews 10:35-36

No discipline is enjoyable while it is happening—it's painful! But afterward there will be a peaceful harvest of right living for those who are trained in this way.

Hebrews 12:11

God has said, "I will never fail you. I will never abandon you."

Hebrews 13:5

FAITH

I tell you the truth, if you had faith even as small as a mustard seed, you could say to this mountain, "Move from here to there," and it would move. Nothing would be impossible.

Matthew 17:20

Have faith in God. I tell you the truth, you can say to this mountain, "May you be lifted up and thrown into the sea," and it will happen. But you must really believe it will happen and have no doubt in your heart.

Mark 11:22-23

Blessed are those who believe without seeing me.

John 20:29

Believe in the Lord Jesus and you will be saved.

Acts 16:31

You are all children of God through faith in Christ Jesus.

Galatians 3:26

God saved you by his grace when you believed. And you can't take credit for this; it is a gift from God.

Ephesians 2:8

Let your roots grow down into him, and let your lives be built on him. Then your faith will grow strong in the truth you were taught, and you will overflow with thankfulness.

Colossians 2:7

Faith is the confidence that what we hope for will actually happen; it gives us assurance about things we cannot see.

Hebrews 11:1

It is impossible to please God without faith. Anyone who wants to come to him must believe that God exists and that he rewards those who sincerely seek him.

Hebrews 11:6

If you need wisdom, ask our generous God, and he will give it to you. He will not rebuke you for asking. But when you ask him, be sure that your faith is in God alone. Do not waver, for a person with divided loyalty is as unsettled as a wave of the sea that is blown and tossed by the wind.

James 1:5-6

When your faith remains strong through many trials, it will bring you much praise and glory and honor on the day when Jesus Christ is revealed to the whole world.

1 Peter 1:7

FAITHFULNESS

God is not a man, so he does not lie. He is not human, so he does not change his mind. Has he ever spoken and failed to act? Has he ever promised and not carried it through?

Numbers 23:19

He is the Rock; his deeds are perfect. Everything he does is just and fair. He is a faithful God who does no wrong; how just and upright he is!

Deuteronomy 32:4

To the faithful you show yourself faithful.

2 Samuel 22:26

O Lord, God of Israel, there is no God like you in all of heaven above or on the earth below. You keep your covenant and show unfailing love to all who walk before you in wholehearted devotion.

1 Kings 8:23

Those who know your name trust in you, for you, O Lord, do not abandon those who search for you.

Psalm 9:10

Surely your goodness and unfailing love will pursue me all the days of my life.

Psalm 23:6

The love of the LORD remains forever with those who fear him. His salvation extends to the children's children of those who are faithful to his covenant, of those who obey his commandments!

Psalm 103:17-18

Your eternal word, O LORD, stands firm in heaven. Your faithfulness extends to every generation, as enduring as the earth you created.

Psalm 119:89-90

"The mountains may move and the hills disappear, but even then my faithful love for you will remain. My covenant of blessing will never be broken," says the LORD, who has mercy on you.

Isaiah 54:10

Great is his faithfulness; his mercies begin afresh each morning.

Lamentations 3:23

I am certain that God, who began the good work within you, will continue his work until it is finally finished on the day when Christ Jesus returns.

Philippians 1:6

The Lord is faithful; he will strengthen you and guard you from the evil one.

2 Thessalonians 3:3

If we are unfaithful, he remains faithful, for he cannot deny who he is.

2 Timothy 2:13

If we are faithful to the end . . . we will share in all that belongs to Christ.

Hebrews 3:14

Let us hold tightly without wavering to the hope we affirm, for God can be trusted to keep his promise.

Hebrews 10:23

Jesus Christ is the same yesterday, today, and forever.

Hebrews 13:8

FAMILY

Honor your father and mother. Then you will live a long, full life in the land the LORD your God is giving you.

Exodus 20:12

How joyful are those who fear the LORD and delight in obeying his commands. Their children will be successful everywhere; an entire generation of godly people will be blessed. They themselves will be wealthy, and their good deeds will last forever.

Psalm 112:1-3

Children are a gift from the LORD; they are a reward from him. Children born to a young man are like arrows in a warrior's hands. How joyful is the man whose quiver is full of them! He will not be put to shame when he confronts his accusers at the city gates.

Psalm 127:3-5

"This is my covenant with them," says the LORD. "My Spirit will not leave them, and neither will these words I have given you. They will be on your lips and on the lips of your children and your children's children forever. I, the LORD, have spoken!"

Isaiah 59:21

Jesus replied, "My mother and my brothers are all those who hear God's word and obey it."

Luke 8:21

God decided in advance to adopt us into his own family by bringing us to himself through Jesus Christ. This is what he wanted to do, and it gave him great pleasure.

Ephesians 1:5

You are members of God's family.

Ephesians 2:19

Children, obey your parents because you belong to the Lord, for this is the right thing to do. "Honor your father and mother." This is the first commandment with a promise: If you honor your father and mother, "things will go well for you, and you will have a long life on the earth."

Ephesians 6:1-3

Those who won't care for their relatives, especially those in their own household, have denied the true faith. Such people are worse than unbelievers.

1 Timothy 5:8

FEAR

Even when I walk through the darkest valley, I will not be afraid, for you are close beside me.

Psalm 23:4

The LORD is my light and my salvation—so why should I be afraid? The LORD is my fortress, protecting me from danger, so why should I tremble? . . . Though a mighty army surrounds me, my heart will not be afraid. Even if I am attacked, I will remain confident.

Psalm 27:1-3

God is our refuge and strength, always ready to help in times of trouble.

Psalm 46:1

He will cover you with his feathers. He will shelter you with his wings. His faithful promises are your armor and protection. Do not be afraid of the terrors of the night, nor the arrow that flies in the day. Do not dread the disease that stalks in darkness, nor the disaster that strikes at midday.

Psalm 91:4-6

Don't be afraid, for I am with you. Don't be discouraged, for I am your God. I will strengthen you and help you. I will hold you up with my victorious right hand.

Isaiah 41:10

I hold you by your right hand—I, the LORD your God. And I say to you, "Don't be afraid. I am here to help you."

Isaiah 41:13

When you go through deep waters, I will be with you. When you go through rivers of difficulty, you will not drown. When you walk through the fire of oppression, you will not be burned up; the flames will not consume you.

Isaiah 43:2

I, yes I, am the one who comforts you. So why are you afraid of mere humans, who wither like the grass and disappear?

Isaiah 51:12

I am leaving you with a gift—peace of mind and heart. And the peace I give is a gift the world cannot give. So don't be troubled or afraid.

John 14:27

If God is for us, who can ever be against us?

Romans 8:31

I am convinced that nothing can ever separate us from God's love. Neither death nor life, neither angels nor demons, neither our fears for today nor our worries about tomorrow—not even the powers of hell can separate us from God's love.

Romans 8:38

God has not given us a spirit of fear and timidity, but of power, love, and self-discipline.

2 Timothy 1:7

We can say with confidence, "The LORD is my helper, so I will have no fear. What can mere people do to me?"

Hebrews 13:6

FINDING GOD

If you search for him with all your heart and soul, you will find him.

Deuteronomy 4:29

If you seek him, you will find him. But if you forsake him, he will reject you forever.

1 Chronicles 28:9

The LORD will stay with you as long as you stay with him! Whenever you seek him, you will find him. But if you abandon him, he will abandon you.

2 Chronicles 15:2

Those who know your name trust in you, for you, O LORD, do not abandon those who search for you.

Psalm 9:10

Seek his will in all you do, and he will show you which path to take.

Proverbs 3:6

I love all who love me. Those who search will surely find me.

Proverbs 8:17

If you look for me wholeheartedly, you will find me.

Jeremiah 29:13

The LORD is good to those who depend on him, to those who search for him.

Lamentations 3:25

Plant the good seeds of righteousness, and you will harvest a crop of love. Plow up the hard ground of your hearts, for now is the time to seek the LORD, that he may come and shower righteousness upon you.

Hosea 10:12

Keep on asking, and you will receive what you ask for. Keep on seeking, and you will find. Keep on knocking, and the door will be opened to you.

Matthew 7:7

His purpose was for the nations to seek after God and perhaps feel their way toward him and find him—though he is not far from any one of us.

Acts 17:27

It is impossible to please God without faith. Anyone who wants to come to him must believe that God exists and that he rewards those who sincerely seek him.

Hebrews 11:6

FORGIVENESS

—— ✺ ——

The LORD is slow to anger and filled with unfailing love, forgiving every kind of sin and rebellion.

Numbers 14:18

I confessed all my sins to you and stopped trying to hide my guilt. I said to myself, "I will confess my rebellion to the LORD." And you forgave me! All my guilt is gone.

Psalm 32:5

O Lord, you are so good, so ready to forgive, so full of unfailing love for all who ask for your help.

Psalm 86:5

Though your sins are like scarlet, I will make them as white as snow.

Isaiah 1:18

I—yes, I alone—will blot out your sins for my own sake and will never think of them again.

Isaiah 43:25

If you forgive those who sin against you, your heavenly Father will forgive you.

Matthew 6:14

I tell you the truth, all sin and blasphemy can be forgiven, but any-one who blasphemes the Holy Spirit will never be forgiven. This is a sin with eternal consequences.

Mark 3:28-29

When you are praying, first forgive anyone you are holding a grudge against, so that your Father in heaven will forgive your sins, too.

Mark 11:25

Do not judge others, and you will not be judged. Do not condemn others, or it will all come back against you. Forgive others, and you will be forgiven.

Luke 6:37

FRUITFULNESS

—— ✤ ——

Oh, the joys of those who do not follow the advice of the wicked, or stand around with sinners, or join in with mockers. But they delight in the law of the LORD, meditating on it day and night. They are like trees planted along the riverbank, bearing fruit each season. Their leaves never wither, and they prosper in all they do.

Psalm 1:1-3

The godly will flourish like palm trees and grow strong like the cedars of Lebanon. For they are transplanted to the LORD's own house. They flourish in the courts of our God. Even in old age they will still produce fruit; they will remain vital and green.

Psalm 92:12-14

I will be to Israel like a refreshing dew from heaven. Israel will blossom like the lily; it will send roots deep into the soil like the cedars in Lebanon. . . . My people will again live under my shade. They will flourish like grain and blossom like grapevines.

Hosea 14:5-7

To those who use well what they are given, even more will be given.

Matthew 25:29

I am the true grapevine, and my Father is the gardener. He cuts off every branch of mine that doesn't produce fruit, and he prunes the branches that do bear fruit so they will produce even more. You have already been pruned and purified by the message I have given you. Remain in me, and I will remain in you. For a branch cannot produce fruit if it is severed from the vine, and you cannot be fruitful unless you remain in me.

John 15:1-4

Yes, I am the vine; you are the branches. Those who remain in me, and I in them, will produce much fruit.

John 15:5

When you produce much fruit, you are my true disciples. This brings great glory to my Father.

John 15:8

May you always be filled with the fruit of your salvation—the righteous character produced in your life by Jesus Christ—for this will bring much glory and praise to God.

Philippians 1:11

This same Good News that came to you is going out all over the world. It is bearing fruit everywhere by changing lives, just as it changed your lives from the day you first heard and understood the truth about God's wonderful grace.

Colossians 1:6

Supplement your faith with a generous provision of moral excellence, and moral excellence with knowledge, and knowledge with self-control, and self-control with patient endurance, and patient endurance with godliness, and godliness with brotherly affection, and brotherly affection with love for everyone. The more you grow like this, the more productive and useful you will be in your knowledge of our Lord Jesus Christ.

2 Peter 1:5-8

FUTURE

The LORD says, "I will guide you along the best pathway for your life. I will advise you and watch over you."

Psalm 32:8

You guide me with your counsel, leading me to a glorious destiny.

Psalm 73:24

"I know the plans I have for you," says the LORD. "They are plans for good and not for disaster, to give you a future and a hope."

Jeremiah 29:11

Don't worry about tomorrow, for tomorrow will bring its own worries. Today's trouble is enough for today.

Matthew 6:34

How do you know what your life will be like tomorrow? Your life is like the morning fog—it's here a little while, then it's gone.

James 4:14

GIVING

———— ⌒⊙⌒ ————

Oh, the joys of those who are kind to the poor! The LORD rescues them when they are in trouble. The LORD protects them and keeps them alive. He gives them prosperity in the land and rescues them from their enemies.

Psalm 41:1-2

Good comes to those who lend money generously and conduct their business fairly. Such people will not be overcome by evil. Those who are righteous will be long remembered.

Psalm 112:5-6

Give freely and become more wealthy; be stingy and lose everything. The generous will prosper; those who refresh others will themselves be refreshed.

Proverbs 11:24-25

If you help the poor, you are lending to the LORD—and he will repay you!

Proverbs 19:17

Feed the hungry, and help those in trouble. Then your light will shine out from the darkness, and the darkness around you will be as bright as noon.

Isaiah 58:10

Give your gifts in private, and your Father, who sees everything, will reward you.

Matthew 6:4

If you give even a cup of cold water to one of the least of my followers, you will surely be rewarded.

Matthew 10:42

Give, and you will receive. Your gift will return to you in full—pressed down, shaken together to make room for more, running over, and poured into your lap. The amount you give will determine the amount you get back.

Luke 6:38

Sell your possessions and give to those in need. This will store up treasure for you in heaven! And the purses of heaven never get old or develop holes. Your treasure will be safe; no thief can steal it and no moth can destroy it.

Luke 12:33

When you put on a luncheon or a banquet . . . invite the poor, the crippled, the lame, and the blind. Then at the resurrection of the righteous, God will reward you for inviting those who could not repay you.

Luke 14:12-14

It is more blessed to give than to receive.

Acts 20:35

You must each decide in your heart how much to give. And don't give reluctantly or in response to pressure. "For God loves a person who gives cheerfully." And God will generously provide all you need. Then you will always have everything you need and plenty left over to share with others.

2 Corinthians 9:7-8

GODLINESS

You bless the godly, O LORD; you surround them with your shield of love.

Psalm 5:12

Tell the godly that all will be well for them. They will enjoy the rich reward they have earned!

Isaiah 3:10

Seek the Kingdom of God above all else, and live righteously, and he will give you everything you need.

Matthew 6:33

We are made right with God by placing our faith in Jesus Christ. And this is true for everyone who believes, no matter who we are.

Romans 3:22

All of us who have had that veil removed can see and reflect the glory of the Lord. And the Lord—who is the Spirit—makes us more and more like him as we are changed into his glorious image.

2 Corinthians 3:18

It is no longer I who live, but Christ lives in me.

Galatians 2:20

GOD'S LOVE

The LORD is slow to anger and filled with unfailing love, forgiving every kind of sin and rebellion.

Numbers 14:18

I lavish unfailing love for a thousand generations on those who love me and obey my commands.

Deuteronomy 5:10

Surely your goodness and unfailing love will pursue me all the days of my life, and I will live in the house of the LORD forever.

Psalm 23:6

I will be glad and rejoice in your unfailing love, for you have seen my troubles, and you care about the anguish of my soul.

Psalm 31:7

He redeems me from death and crowns me with love and tender mercies.

Psalm 103:4

The LORD is compassionate and merciful, slow to get angry and filled with unfailing love.

Psalm 103:8

God loved the world so much that he gave his one and only Son, so that everyone who believes in him will not perish but have eternal life.

John 3:16

Those who accept my commandments and obey them are the ones who love me. And because they love me, my Father will love them. And I will love them and reveal myself to each of them.

John 14:21

This hope will not lead to disappointment. For we know how dearly God loves us, because he has given us the Holy Spirit to fill our hearts with his love.

Romans 5:5

No power in the sky above or in the earth below—indeed, nothing in all creation will ever be able to separate us from the love of God that is revealed in Christ Jesus our Lord.

Romans 8:39

God is so rich in mercy, and he loved us so much, that even though we were dead because of our sins, he gave us life when he raised Christ from the dead.

Ephesians 2:4-5

See how very much our Father loves us, for he calls us his children, and that is what we are!

1 John 3:1

This is real love—not that we loved God, but that he loved us and sent his Son as a sacrifice to take away our sins.

1 John 4:10

We know how much God loves us, and we have put our trust in his love. God is love, and all who live in love live in God, and God lives in them.

1 John 4:16

GOSSIP

How great is the goodness you have stored up for those who fear you. You lavish it on those who come to you for protection, blessing them before the watching world. You hide them in the shelter of your presence, safe from those who conspire against them. You shelter them in your presence, far from accusing tongues.

Psalm 31:19-20

Does anyone want to live a life that is long and prosperous? Then keep your tongue from speaking evil and your lips from telling lies!

Psalm 34:12-13

He will send help from heaven to rescue me, disgracing those who hound me.

Psalm 57:3

A gossip goes around telling secrets, but those who are trustworthy can keep a confidence.

Proverbs 11:13

As surely as a north wind brings rain, so a gossiping tongue causes anger!

Proverbs 25:23

God blesses you when people mock you and persecute you and lie about you and say all sorts of evil things against you because you are my followers. Be happy about it! Be very glad! For a great reward awaits you in heaven.

Matthew 5:11-12

Be happy when you are insulted for being a Christian, for then the glorious Spirit of God rests upon you.

1 Peter 4:14

GROWTH

The righteous keep moving forward, and those with clean hands become stronger and stronger.

Job 17:9

The way of the righteous is like the first gleam of dawn, which shines ever brighter until the full light of day.

Proverbs 4:18

All of us who have had that veil removed can see and reflect the glory of the Lord. And the Lord—who is the Spirit—makes us more and more like him as we are changed into his glorious image.

2 Corinthians 3:18

I am certain that God, who began the good work within you, will continue his work until it is finally finished on the day when Christ Jesus returns.

Philippians 1:6

Forgetting the past and looking forward to what lies ahead, I press on to reach the end of the race and receive the heavenly prize for which God, through Christ Jesus, is calling us.

Philippians 3:13-14

We ask God to give you complete knowledge of his will and to give you spiritual wisdom and understanding. Then the way you live will always honor and please the Lord, and your lives will produce every kind of good fruit. All the while, you will grow as you learn to know God better and better.

Colossians 1:9-10

GUIDANCE

The LORD is good and does what is right; he shows the proper path to those who go astray.

Psalm 25:8

The LORD says, "I will guide you along the best pathway for your life. I will advise you and watch over you."

Psalm 32:8

The LORD directs the steps of the godly. He delights in every detail of their lives.

Psalm 37:23

That is what God is like. He is our God forever and ever, and he will guide us until we die.

Psalm 48:14

I still belong to you; you hold my right hand. You guide me with your counsel, leading me to a glorious destiny.

Psalm 73:23-24

The LORD will work out his plans for my life—for your faithful love, O LORD, endures forever. Don't abandon me, for you made me.

Psalm 138:8

My child, listen to what I say, and treasure my commands. . . . Then you will understand what is right, just, and fair, and you will find the right way to go.

Proverbs 2:1, 9

Seek his will in all you do, and he will show you which path to take.

Proverbs 3:6

We can make our plans, but the LORD determines our steps.

Proverbs 16:9

"I know the plans I have for you," says the LORD. "They are plans for good and not for disaster, to give you a future and a hope."

Jeremiah 29:11

I am the light of the world. If you follow me, you won't have to walk in darkness, because you will have the light that leads to life.

John 8:12

If you need wisdom, ask our generous God, and he will give it to you. He will not rebuke you for asking. But when you ask him, be sure that your faith is in God alone. Do not waver, for a person with divided loyalty is as unsettled as a wave of the sea that is blown and tossed by the wind.

James 1:5-6

GUILT

—— ∽⊙⌒ ——

Those who look to him for help will be radiant with joy; no shadow of shame will darken their faces.

Psalm 34:5

Purify me from my sins, and I will be clean; wash me, and I will be whiter than snow.

Psalm 51:7

He has removed our sins as far from us as the east is from the west.

Psalm 103:12

I—yes, I alone—will blot out your sins for my own sake and will never think of them again.

Isaiah 43:25

Let the wicked change their ways and banish the very thought of doing wrong. Let them turn to the LORD that he may have mercy on them. Yes, turn to our God, for he will forgive generously.

Isaiah 55:7

I will cleanse them of their sins against me and forgive all their sins of rebellion.

Jeremiah 33:8

Everyone who believes in him is declared right with God.

Acts 13:39

Everyone has sinned; we all fall short of God's glorious standard. Yet God, with undeserved kindness, declares that we are righteous. He did this through Christ Jesus when he freed us from the penalty for our sins.

Romans 3:23-24

This means that anyone who belongs to Christ has become a new person. The old life is gone; a new life has begun!

2 Corinthians 5:17

I will forgive their wickedness, and I will never again remember their sins.

Hebrews 8:12

If we confess our sins to him, he is faithful and just to forgive us our sins and to cleanse us from all wickedness.

1 John 1:9

Even if we feel guilty, God is greater than our feelings, and he knows everything.

1 John 3:20

HELP FROM GOD

―――― ❦ ――――

Is anything too hard for the LORD?

Genesis 18:14

He has not ignored or belittled the suffering of the needy. He has not turned his back on them, but has listened to their cries for help.

Psalm 22:24

Commit everything you do to the LORD. Trust him, and he will help you.

Psalm 37:5

Though they stumble, they will never fall, for the LORD holds them by the hand.

Psalm 37:24

My health may fail, and my spirit may grow weak, but God remains the strength of my heart; he is mine forever.

Psalm 73:26

The LORD helps the fallen and lifts those bent beneath their loads.

Psalm 145:14

As for me, I look to the LORD for help. I wait confidently for God to save me, and my God will certainly hear me.

Micah 7:7

We can say with confidence, "The LORD is my helper, so I will have no fear. What can mere people do to me?"

Hebrews 13:6

HOLY SPIRIT

I will sprinkle clean water on you, and you will be clean. Your filth will be washed away, and you will no longer worship idols. And I will give you a new heart, and I will put a new spirit in you. I will take out your stony, stubborn heart and give you a tender, responsive heart. And I will put my Spirit in you so that you will follow my decrees and be careful to obey my regulations.

Ezekiel 36:25-27

When you are brought to trial in the synagogues and before rulers and authorities, don't worry about how to defend yourself or what to say, for the Holy Spirit will teach you at that time what needs to be said.

Luke 12:11-12

I will ask the Father, and he will give you another Advocate, who will never leave you. He is the Holy Spirit, who leads into all truth. The world cannot receive him, because it isn't looking for him and doesn't recognize him. But you know him, because he lives with you now and later will be in you.

John 14:16-17

When the Father sends the Advocate as my representative—that is, the Holy Spirit—he will teach you everything and will remind you of everything I have told you.

John 14:26

When the Spirit of truth comes, he will guide you into all truth.

John 16:13

You will receive power when the Holy Spirit comes upon you. And you will be my witnesses, telling people about me everywhere.

Acts 1:8

The Holy Spirit helps us in our weakness. For example, we don't know what God wants us to pray for. But the Holy Spirit prays for us with groanings that cannot be expressed in words. And the Father who knows all hearts knows what the Spirit is saying, for the Spirit pleads for us believers in harmony with God's own will.

Romans 8:26-27

We have received God's Spirit (not the world's spirit), so we can know the wonderful things God has freely given us.

1 Corinthians 2:12

The Spirit is God's guarantee that he will give us the inheritance he promised and that he has purchased us to be his own people.

Ephesians 1:14

You have received the Holy Spirit, and he lives within you, so you don't need anyone to teach you what is true. For the Spirit teaches you everything you need to know, and what he teaches is true—it is not a lie. So just as he has taught you, remain in fellowship with Christ.

1 John 2:27

Those who obey God's commandments remain in fellowship with him, and he with them. And we know he lives in us because the Spirit he gave us lives in us.

1 John 3:24

HONESTY

—— ❧❦ ——

Who may stand in his holy place? Only those whose hands and hearts are pure, who do not worship idols and never tell lies. They will receive the LORD's blessing and have a right relationship with God their savior.

Psalm 24:3-5

Yes, what joy for those whose record the LORD has cleared of guilt, whose lives are lived in complete honesty!

Psalm 32:2

The wicked borrow and never repay, but the godly are generous givers.

Psalm 37:21

Look at those who are honest and good, for a wonderful future awaits those who love peace.

Psalm 37:37

Honesty guides good people; dishonesty destroys treacherous people. . . . The godly are directed by honesty; the wicked fall beneath their load of sin.

Proverbs 11:3-5

Truthful words stand the test of time, but lies are soon exposed.

Proverbs 12:19

A false witness will not go unpunished, nor will a liar escape.

Proverbs 19:5

The commandments say, "You must not commit adultery. You must not murder. You must not steal. You must not covet." These—and other such commandments—are summed up in this one commandment: "Love your neighbor as yourself." Love does no wrong to others, so love fulfills the requirements of God's law.

Romans 13:9-10

Cowards, unbelievers, the corrupt, murderers, the immoral, those who practice witchcraft, idol worshipers, and all liars— their fate is in the fiery lake of burning sulfur.

Revelation 21:8

HOPE

—— ∾ ❧ ——

Having hope will give you courage.

Job 11:18

Why am I discouraged? Why is my heart so sad? I will put my hope in God! I will praise him again—my Savior and my God!

Psalm 42:11

When doubts filled my mind, your comfort gave me renewed hope and cheer.

Psalm 94:19

Hope in the LORD; for with the LORD there is unfailing love. His redemption overflows.

Psalm 130:7

"I know the plans I have for you," says the LORD. "They are plans for good and not for disaster, to give you a future and a hope."

Jeremiah 29:11

I pray that God, the source of hope, will fill you completely with joy and peace because you trust in him. Then you will overflow with confident hope through the power of the Holy Spirit.

Romans 15:13

This is the secret: Christ lives in you. This gives you assurance of sharing his glory.

Colossians 1:27

Let us hold tightly without wavering to the hope we affirm, for God can be trusted to keep his promise.

Hebrews 10:23

Be truly glad. There is wonderful joy ahead, even though you have to endure many trials for a little while.

1 Peter 1:6

Through Christ you have come to trust in God. And you have placed your faith and hope in God because he raised Christ from the dead and gave him great glory.

1 Peter 1:21

HUMILITY

—— ∽◎⌒ ——

You rescue the humble, but your eyes watch the proud and humiliate them.

2 Samuel 22:28

You rescue the humble, but you humiliate the proud.

Psalm 18:27

He leads the humble in doing right, teaching them his way.

Psalm 25:9

The humble will see their God at work and be glad. Let all who seek God's help be encouraged.

Psalm 69:32

Though the LORD is great, he cares for the humble, but he keeps his distance from the proud.

Psalm 138:6

The LORD delights in his people; he crowns the humble with victory.

Psalm 149:4

Fear of the LORD teaches wisdom; humility precedes honor.

Proverbs 15:33

The humble will be filled with fresh joy from the LORD. The poor will rejoice in the Holy One of Israel.

Isaiah 29:19

I live in the high and holy place with those whose spirits are contrite and humble. I restore the crushed spirit of the humble and revive the courage of those with repentant hearts.

Isaiah 57:15

God blesses those who are humble, for they will inherit the whole earth.

Matthew 5:5

Anyone who becomes as humble as this little child is the greatest in the Kingdom of Heaven.

Matthew 18:4

JEALOUSY

Don't worry about the wicked or envy those who do wrong. For like grass, they soon fade away. Like spring flowers, they soon wither.

Psalm 37:1-2

Thieves are jealous of each other's loot, but the godly are well rooted and bear their own fruit.

Proverbs 12:12

Don't envy sinners, but always continue to fear the LORD. You will be rewarded for this; your hope will not be disappointed.

Proverbs 23:17-18

Anger is cruel, and wrath is like a flood, but jealousy is even more dangerous.

Proverbs 27:4

I observed that most people are motivated to success because they envy their neighbors. But this, too, is meaningless—like chasing the wind.

Ecclesiastes 4:4

Wherever there is jealousy and selfish ambition, there you will find disorder and evil of every kind.

James 3:16

JESUS CHRIST

———— ∽◎◎ ————

God loved the world so much that he gave his one and only Son, so that everyone who believes in him will not perish but have eternal life. God sent his Son into the world not to judge the world, but to save the world through him.

John 3:16-17

Believe in the Lord Jesus and you will be saved.

Acts 16:31

God promised this Good News long ago through his prophets in the holy Scriptures. The Good News is about his Son.

Romans 1:2-3

You see, just as death came into the world through a man, now the resurrection from the dead has begun through another man. Just as everyone dies because we all belong to Adam, everyone who belongs to Christ will be given new life.

1 Corinthians 15:21-22

He has enabled you to share in the inheritance that belongs to his people, who live in the light. For he has rescued us from the kingdom of darkness and transferred us into the Kingdom of his dear Son, who purchased our freedom and forgave our sins.

Colossians 1:12-14

Christ is the visible image of the invisible God.

Colossians 1:15

He existed before anything else, and he holds all creation together.

Colossians 1:17

You who were once far away from God . . . were his enemies, separated from him by your evil thoughts and actions. Yet now he has reconciled you to himself through the death of Christ in his physical body. As a result, he has brought you into his own presence, and you are holy and blameless as you stand before him without a single fault.

Colossians 1:21-22

JOY

The joy of the LORD is your strength!

Nehemiah 8:10

You have given me greater joy than those who have abundant harvests of grain and new wine.

Psalm 4:7

I will be filled with joy because of you. I will sing praises to your name, O Most High.

Psalm 9:2

You will show me the way of life, granting me the joy of your presence and the pleasures of living with you forever.

Psalm 16:11

His anger lasts only a moment, but his favor lasts a lifetime! Weeping may last through the night, but joy comes with the morning.

Psalm 30:5

In him our hearts rejoice, for we trust in his holy name.

Psalm 33:21

Those who look to him for help will be radiant with joy; no shadow of shame will darken their faces. . . . Taste and see that the LORD is good. Oh, the joys of those who take refuge in him!

Psalm 34:5, 8

Happy are those who hear the joyful call to worship, for they will walk in the light of your presence, LORD. They rejoice all day long in your wonderful reputation. They exult in your righteousness.

Psalm 89:15-16

Light shines on the godly, and joy on those whose hearts are right.

Psalm 97:11

Those who plant in tears will harvest with shouts of joy. They weep as they go to plant their seed, but they sing as they return with the harvest.

Psalm 126:5-6

How joyful are those who fear the LORD—all who follow his ways!

Psalm 128:1

You will live in joy and peace. The mountains and hills will burst into song, and the trees of the field will clap their hands!

Isaiah 55:12

I am overwhelmed with joy in the LORD my God! For he has dressed me with the clothing of salvation and draped me in a robe of righteousness. I am like a bridegroom in his wedding suit or a bride with her jewels.

Isaiah 61:10

You have sorrow now, but I will see you again; then you will rejoice, and no one can rob you of that joy.

John 16:22

You love him even though you have never seen him. Though you do not see him now, you trust him; and you rejoice with a glorious, inexpressible joy.

1 Peter 1:8

All glory to God, who is able to keep you from falling away and will bring you with great joy into his glorious presence without a single fault.

Jude 1:24

LAZINESS

Work hard and become a leader; be lazy and become a slave.

Proverbs 12:24

Lazy people want much but get little, but those who work hard will prosper.

Proverbs 13:4

Good planning and hard work lead to prosperity, but hasty short-cuts lead to poverty.

Proverbs 21:5

Know the state of your flocks, and put your heart into caring for your herds.

Proverbs 27:23

To those who use well what they are given, even more will be given, and they will have an abundance. But from those who do nothing, even what little they have will be taken away.

Matthew 25:29

Remember this—a farmer who plants only a few seeds will get a small crop. But the one who plants generously will get a generous crop.

2 Corinthians 9:6

Make it your goal to live a quiet life, minding your own business and working with your hands, just as we instructed you before. Then people who are not Christians will respect the way you live, and you will not need to depend on others.

1 Thessalonians 4:11-12

LIVING FOR GOD

—— ✧ ——

Stay on the path that the LORD your God has commanded you to follow. Then you will live long and prosperous lives in the land you are about to enter and occupy.

Deuteronomy 5:33

If you obey all his decrees and commands, you will enjoy a long life.

Deuteronomy 6:2

O God, you have taught me from my earliest childhood, and I constantly tell others about the wonderful things you do. Now that I am old and gray, do not abandon me, O God. Let me proclaim your power to this new generation, your mighty miracles to all who come after me.

Psalm 71:17-18

The LORD says, "I will rescue those who love me. I will protect those who trust in my name. . . . I will reward them with a long life and give them my salvation."

Psalm 91:14-16

Even in old age they will still produce fruit; they will remain vital and green. They will declare, "The LORD is just! He is my rock! There is no evil in him!"

Psalm 92:14-15

My child, never forget the things I have taught you. Store my commands in your heart. If you do this, you will live many years, and your life will be satisfying.

Proverbs 3:1-2

I will be your God throughout your lifetime—until your hair is white with age. I made you, and I will care for you. I will carry you along and save you.

Isaiah 46:4

LONELINESS

———— ❧ ❦ ————

I am with you, and I will protect you wherever you go. . . . I will not leave you until I have finished giving you everything I have promised you.

Genesis 28:15

I will walk among you; I will be your God, and you will be my people.

Leviticus 26:12

The LORD your God is with you wherever you go.

Joshua 1:9

I know the LORD is always with me. I will not be shaken, for he is right beside me. . . . You will show me the way of life, granting me the joy of your presence and the pleasures of living with you forever.

Psalm 16:8, 11

Even when I walk through the darkest valley . . . you are close beside me.

Psalm 23:4

When you go through deep waters, I will be with you.

Isaiah 43:2

When you call, the LORD will answer. "Yes, I am here," he will quickly reply.

Isaiah 58:9

LOVING GOD

—— ～⊚ ⊚～ ——

Take delight in the LORD, and he will give you your heart's desires. Commit everything you do to the LORD. Trust him, and he will help you.

Psalm 37:4-5

The LORD says, "I will rescue those who love me. I will protect those who trust in my name."

Psalm 91:14

The LORD protects all those who love him, but he destroys the wicked.

Psalm 145:20

I love all who love me. Those who search will surely find me.

Proverbs 8:17

Those who love me inherit wealth. I will fill their treasuries.

Proverbs 8:21

Those who accept my commandments and obey them are the ones who love me. And because they love me, my Father will love them. And I will love them and reveal myself to each of them.

John 14:21

No eye has seen, no ear has heard, and no mind has imagined what God has prepared for those who love him.

1 Corinthians 2:9

LOVING OTHERS

———— ✺ ————

I am giving you a new commandment: Love each other. Just as I have loved you, you should love each other. Your love for one another will prove to the world that you are my disciples.

John 13:34-35

Since God chose you to be the holy people he loves, you must clothe yourselves with tenderhearted mercy, kindness, humility, gentleness, and patience. Make allowance for each other's faults, and forgive anyone who offends you. Remember, the Lord forgave you, so you must forgive others.

Colossians 3:12-13

We don't need to write to you about the importance of loving each other, for God himself has taught you to love one another.

1 Thessalonians 4:9

God is not unjust. He will not forget how hard you have worked for him and how you have shown your love to him by caring for other believers, as you still do.

Hebrews 6:10

Anyone who loves another brother or sister is living in the light and does not cause others to stumble.

1 John 2:10

Dear friends, let us continue to love one another, for love comes from God. Anyone who loves is a child of God and knows God. But anyone who does not love does not know God, for God is love.

1 John 4:7-8

We love each other because he loved us first.

1 John 4:19

MARRIAGE

Your wife will be like a fruitful grapevine, flourishing within your home. Your children will be like vigorous young olive trees as they sit around your table. That is the LORD's blessing for those who fear him.

Psalm 128:3-4

Husbands ought to love their wives as they love their own bodies. For a man who loves his wife actually shows love for himself.

Ephesians 5:28

As the Scriptures say, "A man leaves his father and mother and is joined to his wife, and the two are united into one."

Ephesians 5:31

These older women must train the younger women to love their husbands and their children, to live wisely and be pure, to work in their homes, to do good, and to be submissive to their husbands. Then they will not bring shame on the word of God.

Titus 2:4-5

Give honor to marriage, and remain faithful to one another in marriage. God will surely judge people who are immoral and those who commit adultery.

Hebrews 13:4

You husbands must give honor to your wives. Treat your wife with understanding as you live together. She may be weaker than you are, but she is your equal partner in God's gift of new life. Treat her as you should so your prayers will not be hindered.

1 Peter 3:7

MERCY

The LORD is compassionate and merciful, slow to get angry and filled with unfailing love.

Psalm 103:8

For my own sake and for the honor of my name, I will hold back my anger and not wipe you out.

Isaiah 48:9

In all their suffering he also suffered, and he personally rescued them. In his love and mercy he redeemed them. He lifted them up and carried them through all the years.

Isaiah 63:9

The faithful love of the LORD never ends! His mercies never cease. Great is his faithfulness; his mercies begin afresh each morning.

Lamentations 3:22-23

Return to the LORD your God, for he is merciful and compassionate, slow to get angry and filled with unfailing love. He is eager to relent and not punish.

Joel 2:13

I promise this very day that I will repay two blessings for each of your troubles.

Zechariah 9:12

God blesses those who are merciful, for they will be shown mercy.

Matthew 5:7

He shows mercy from generation to generation to all who fear him.

Luke 1:50

All praise to God, the Father of our Lord Jesus Christ. God is our merciful Father and the source of all comfort.

2 Corinthians 1:3

God is so rich in mercy, and he loved us so much, that even though we were dead because of our sins, he gave us life when he raised Christ from the dead.

Ephesians 2:4-5

Let us come boldly to the throne of our gracious God. There we will receive his mercy, and we will find grace to help us when we need it most.

Hebrews 4:16

MONEY

Remember the LORD your God. He is the one who gives you power to be successful, in order to fulfill the covenant he confirmed to your ancestors with an oath.

Deuteronomy 8:18

Give generously to the poor, not grudgingly, for the LORD your God will bless you in everything you do.

Deuteronomy 15:10

Riches won't help on the day of judgment, but right living can save you from death.

Proverbs 11:4

Don't wear yourself out trying to get rich. Be wise enough to know when to quit. In the blink of an eye wealth disappears, for it will sprout wings and fly away like an eagle.

Proverbs 23:4-5

Those who love money will never have enough. How meaningless to think that wealth brings true happiness!

Ecclesiastes 5:10

Send your grain across the seas, and in time, profits will flow back to you. But divide your investments among many places, for you do not know what risks might lie ahead.

Ecclesiastes 11:1-2

"Bring all the tithes into the storehouse so there will be enough food in my Temple. If you do," says the LORD of Heaven's Armies, "I will open the windows of heaven for you. I will pour out a blessing so great you won't have enough room to take it in! Try it! Put me to the test!"

Malachi 3:10

When you give to someone in need, don't let your left hand know what your right hand is doing. Give your gifts in private, and your Father, who sees everything, will reward you.

Matthew 6:3-4

Don't store up treasures here on earth, where moths eat them and rust destroys them, and where thieves break in and steal. Store your treasures in heaven, where moths and rust cannot destroy, and thieves do not break in and steal. Wherever your treasure is, there the desires of your heart will also be.

Matthew 6:19-21

No one can serve two masters. For you will hate one and love the other; you will be devoted to one and despise the other. You cannot serve both God and money.

Matthew 6:24

Don't worry about these things, saying, "What will we eat? What will we drink? What will we wear?" These things dominate the thoughts of unbelievers, but your heavenly Father already knows all your needs. Seek the Kingdom of God above all else, and live righteously, and he will give you everything you need.

Matthew 6:31-33

Everyone who has given up houses or brothers or sisters or father or mother or children or property, for my sake, will receive a hundred times as much in return and will inherit eternal life.

Matthew 19:29

To those who use well what they are given, even more will be given, and they will have an abundance. But from those who do nothing, even what little they have will be taken away.

Matthew 25:29

Give, and you will receive. Your gift will return to you in full— pressed down, shaken together to make room for more, running over, and poured into your lap. The amount you give will determine the amount you get back.

Luke 6:38

Sell your possessions and give to those in need. This will store up treasure for you in heaven! And the purses of heaven never get old or develop holes. Your treasure will be safe; no thief can steal it and no moth can destroy it.

Luke 12:33

You must each decide in your heart how much to give. And don't give reluctantly or in response to pressure. "For God loves a person who gives cheerfully."

2 Corinthians 9:7

Teach those who are rich in this world not to be proud and not to trust in their money, which is so unreliable. Their trust should be in God, who richly gives us all we need for our enjoyment.

1 Timothy 6:17

Listen to me, dear brothers and sisters. Hasn't God chosen the poor in this world to be rich in faith? Aren't they the ones who will inherit the Kingdom he promised to those who love him?

James 2:5

NEEDS

The LORD is my shepherd; I have all that I need. He lets me rest in green meadows; he leads me beside peaceful streams. He renews my strength. He guides me along right paths, bringing honor to his name.

Psalm 23:1-3

He gives food to those who fear him; he always remembers his covenant.

Psalm 111:5

The LORD himself watches over you! The LORD stands beside you as your protective shade. The sun will not harm you by day, nor the moon at night.

Psalm 121:5-6

Your heavenly Father already knows all your needs. Seek the Kingdom of God above all else, and live righteously, and he will give you everything you need.

Matthew 6:32-33

Look at the lilies and how they grow. They don't work or make their clothing, yet Solomon in all his glory was not dressed as beautifully as they are. And if God cares so wonderfully for flowers that are here today and thrown into the fire tomorrow, he will certainly care for you.

Luke 12:27-28

Don't worry about anything; instead, pray about everything. Tell God what you need, and thank him for all he has done. Then you will experience God's peace, which exceeds anything we can understand.

Philippians 4:6-7

This same God who takes care of me will supply all your needs from his glorious riches, which have been given to us in Christ Jesus.

Philippians 4:19

By his divine power, God has given us everything we need for living a godly life. We have received all of this by coming to know him, the one who called us to himself by means of his marvelous glory and excellence.

2 Peter 1:3

OBEDIENCE

Do what is right and good in the LORD's sight, so all will go well with you.

Deuteronomy 6:18

Look, today I am giving you the choice between a blessing and a curse! You will be blessed if you obey the commands of the LORD your God that I am giving you today. But you will be cursed if you reject the commands of the LORD your God and turn away from him.

Deuteronomy 11:26-28

The LORD God is our sun and our shield. He gives us grace and glory. The LORD will withhold no good thing from those who do what is right.

Psalm 84:11

Joyful are those who obey his laws and search for him with all their hearts.

Psalm 119:2

Oh, that my actions would consistently reflect your decrees! Then I will not be ashamed when I compare my life with your commands. As I learn your righteous regulations, I will thank you by living as I should!

Psalm 119:5-7

Anyone who listens to my teaching and follows it is wise, like a person who builds a house on solid rock. Though the rain comes in torrents and the floodwaters rise and the winds beat against that house, it won't collapse because it is built on bedrock.

Matthew 7:24-25

I tell you the truth, anyone who obeys my teaching will never die!

John 8:51

If you love me, obey my commandments. And I will ask the Father, and he will give you another Advocate, who will never leave you.

John 14:15-16

When you obey my commandments, you remain in my love, just as I obey my Father's commandments and remain in his love.

John 15:10

Merely listening to the law doesn't make us right with God. It is obeying the law that makes us right in his sight

Romans 2:13

God is working in you, giving you the desire and the power to do what pleases him.

Philippians 2:13

Keep putting into practice all you learned and received from me—everything you heard from me and saw me doing. Then the God of peace will be with you.

Philippians 4:9

I will put my laws in their minds, and I will write them on their hearts. I will be their God, and they will be my people.

Hebrews 8:10

If you look carefully into the perfect law that sets you free, and if you do what it says and don't forget what you heard, then God will bless you for doing it.

James 1:25

We can be sure that we know him if we obey his commandments.

1 John 2:3

This world is fading away, along with everything that people crave. But anyone who does what pleases God will live forever.

1 John 2:17

We will receive from him whatever we ask because we obey him and do the things that please him.

1 John 3:22

Those who obey God's commandments remain in fellowship with him, and he with them. And we know he lives in us because the Spirit he gave us lives in us.

1 John 3:24

PATIENCE

I waited patiently for the LORD to help me, and he turned to me and heard my cry.

Psalm 40:1

The LORD must wait for you to come to him so he can show you his love and compassion. For the LORD is a faithful God. Blessed are those who wait for his help.

Isaiah 30:18

Those who trust in the LORD will find new strength. They will soar high on wings like eagles. They will run and not grow weary. They will walk and not faint.

Isaiah 40:31

This vision is for a future time. It describes the end, and it will be fulfilled. If it seems slow in coming, wait patiently, for it will surely take place. It will not be delayed.

Habakkuk 2:3

Even though God has the right to show his anger and his power, he is very patient with those on whom his anger falls.

Romans 9:22

The Scriptures give us hope and encouragement as we wait patiently for God's promises to be fulfilled. May God, who gives this patience and encouragement, help you live in complete harmony with each other, as is fitting for followers of Christ Jesus.

Romans 15:4-5

Love is patient and kind.

1 Corinthians 13:4

The Holy Spirit produces this kind of fruit in our lives: love, joy, peace, patience, kindness, goodness, faithfulness, gentleness, and self-control.

Galatians 5:22-23

Let's not get tired of doing what is good. At just the right time we will reap a harvest of blessing if we don't give up.

Galatians 6:9

Patient endurance is what you need now, so that you will continue to do God's will. Then you will receive all that he has promised.

Hebrews 10:36

God blesses those who patiently endure testing and temptation. Afterward they will receive the crown of life that God has promised to those who love him.

James 1:12

Dear brothers and sisters, be patient as you wait for the Lord's return. Consider the farmers who patiently wait for the rains in the fall and in the spring. They eagerly look for the valuable harvest to ripen. You, too, must be patient. Take courage, for the coming of the Lord is near.

James 5:7-8

Of course, you get no credit for being patient if you are beaten for doing wrong. But if you suffer for doing good and endure it patiently, God is pleased with you.

1 Peter 2:20

Make every effort to respond to God's promises. Supplement your faith with a generous provision of moral excellence, and moral excellence with knowledge, and knowledge with self-control, and self-control with patient endurance, and patient endurance with godliness, and godliness with brotherly affection, and brotherly affection with love for everyone. The more you grow like this, the more productive and useful you will be in your knowledge of our Lord Jesus Christ. But those who fail to develop in this way are shortsighted or blind, forgetting that they have been cleansed from their old sins.

2 Peter 1:5-9

PEACE

In peace I will lie down and sleep, for you alone, O LORD, will keep me safe.

Psalm 4:8

Look at those who are honest and good, for a wonderful future awaits those who love peace.

Psalm 37:37

Those who love your instructions have great peace and do not stumble.

Psalm 119:165

You will keep in perfect peace all who trust in you, all whose thoughts are fixed on you!

Isaiah 26:3

This righteousness will bring peace. Yes, it will bring quietness and confidence forever.

Isaiah 32:17

Oh, that you had listened to my commands! Then you would have had peace flowing like a gentle river and righteousness rolling over you like waves in the sea.

Isaiah 48:18

God blesses those who work for peace, for they will be called the children of God.

Matthew 5:9

I am leaving you with a gift—peace of mind and heart. And the peace I give is a gift the world cannot give. So don't be troubled or afraid.

John 14:27

The Holy Spirit produces this kind of fruit in our lives: love, joy, peace, patience, kindness, goodness, faithfulness, gentleness, and self-control.

Galatians 5:22-23

Don't worry about anything; instead, pray about everything. Tell God what you need, and thank him for all he has done. Then you will experience God's peace, which exceeds anything we can understand. His peace will guard your hearts and minds as you live in Christ Jesus.

Philippians 4:6-7

PRAYER

He does not ignore the cries of those who suffer.

Psalm 9:12

The LORD hears his people when they call to him for help. He rescues them from all their troubles.

Psalm 34:17

Call on me when you are in trouble, and I will rescue you, and you will give me glory.

Psalm 50:15

Morning, noon, and night I cry out in my distress, and the LORD hears my voice.

Psalm 55:17

Give your burdens to the LORD, and he will take care of you. He will not permit the godly to slip and fall.

Psalm 55:22

When they call on me, I will answer; I will be with them in trouble. I will rescue and honor them.

Psalm 91:15

As soon as I pray, you answer me; you encourage me by giving me strength.

Psalm 138:3

The LORD is close to all who call on him, yes, to all who call on him in truth.

Psalm 145:18

The LORD is far from the wicked, but he hears the prayers of the righteous.

Proverbs 15:29

When you call, the LORD will answer. "Yes, I am here," he will quickly reply.

Isaiah 58:9

I will answer them before they even call to me. While they are still talking about their needs, I will go ahead and answer their prayers!

Isaiah 65:24

When you pray, go away by yourself, shut the door behind you, and pray to your Father in private. Then your Father, who sees everything, will reward you.

Matthew 6:6

Your Father knows exactly what you need even before you ask him.

Matthew 6:8

Keep on asking, and you will receive what you ask for.

Matthew 7:7

You can pray for anything, and if you have faith, you will receive it.

Matthew 21:22

I tell you, you can pray for anything, and if you believe that you've received it, it will be yours.

Mark 11:24

If you remain in me and my words remain in you, you may ask for anything you want, and it will be granted!

John 15:7

Ask, using my name, and you will receive, and you will have abundant joy.

John 16:24

Don't worry about anything; instead, pray about everything. Tell God what you need, and thank him for all he has done. Then you will experience God's peace, which exceeds anything we can understand. His peace will guard your hearts and minds as you live in Christ Jesus.

Philippians 4:6-7

The earnest prayer of a righteous person has great power and produces wonderful results.

James 5:16

The eyes of the Lord watch over those who do right, and his ears are open to their prayers.

1 Peter 3:12

Give all your worries and cares to God, for he cares about you.

1 Peter 5:7

We are confident that he hears us whenever we ask for anything that pleases him. And since we know he hears us when we make our requests, we also know that he will give us what we ask for.

1 John 5:14-15

PRIDE

You rebuke the arrogant; those who wander from your commands are cursed.

Psalm 119:21

Trust in the LORD with all your heart; do not depend on your own understanding. Seek his will in all you do, and he will show you which path to take. Don't be impressed with your own wisdom. Instead, fear the LORD and turn away from evil.

Proverbs 3:5-7

The LORD mocks the mockers but is gracious to the humble.

Proverbs 3:34

Pride goes before destruction, and haughtiness before a fall.

Proverbs 16:18

Those who trust their own insight are foolish, but anyone who walks in wisdom is safe.

Proverbs 28:26

Pride ends in humiliation, while humility brings honor.

Proverbs 29:23

What sorrow for those who are wise in their own eyes and think themselves so clever.

Isaiah 5:21

We are all infected and impure with sin. When we display our righteous deeds, they are nothing but filthy rags. Like autumn leaves, we wither and fall, and our sins sweep us away like the wind.

Isaiah 64:6

Those who exalt themselves will be humbled, and those who humble themselves will be exalted.

Matthew 23:12

He sat down, called the twelve disciples over to him, and said, "Whoever wants to be first must take last place and be the servant of everyone else."

Mark 9:35

If you think you are too important to help someone, you are only fooling yourself. You are not that important.

Galatians 6:3

If you are wise and understand God's ways, prove it by living an honorable life, doing good works with the humility that comes from wisdom.

James 3:13

Humble yourselves under the mighty power of God, and at the right time he will lift you up in honor.

1 Peter 5:6

PROTECTION

He will protect his faithful ones, but the wicked will disappear in darkness. No one will succeed by strength alone.

1 Samuel 2:9

In peace I will lie down and sleep, for you alone, O LORD, will keep me safe.

Psalm 4:8

The LORD is a shelter for the oppressed, a refuge in times of trouble.

Psalm 9:9

God's way is perfect. All the LORD's promises prove true. He is a shield for all who look to him for protection.

Psalm 18:30

Even when I walk through the darkest valley, I will not be afraid, for you are close beside me. Your rod and your staff protect and comfort me.

Psalm 23:4

The LORD is my light and my salvation—so why should I be afraid? The LORD is my fortress, protecting me from danger, so why should I tremble?

Psalm 27:1

Those who live in the shelter of the Most High will find rest in the shadow of the Almighty. This I declare about the LORD: He alone is my refuge, my place of safety; he is my God, and I trust him. For he will rescue you from every trap and protect you from deadly disease. He will cover you with his feathers. He will shelter you with his wings. His faithful promises are your armor and protection.

Psalm 91:1-4

If you make the LORD your refuge, if you make the Most High your shelter, no evil will conquer you.

Psalm 91:9-10

He will order his angels to protect you wherever you go.

Psalm 91:11

The LORD says, "I will rescue those who love me. I will protect those who trust in my name. When they call on me, I will answer; I will be with them in trouble. I will rescue and honor them. I will reward them with a long life and give them my salvation."

Psalm 91:14-16

The LORD . . . watches over your life. The LORD keeps watch over you as you come and go, both now and forever.

Psalm 121:7-8

The LORD protects all those who love him, but he destroys the wicked.

Psalm 145:20

The name of the LORD is a strong fortress; the godly run to him and are safe.

Proverbs 18:10

Do not be afraid, for I have ransomed you. I have called you by name; you are mine. When you go through deep waters, I will be with you. When you go through rivers of difficulty, you will not drown. When you walk through the fire of oppression, you will not be burned up; the flames will not consume you.

Isaiah 43:1-2

The Lord is faithful; he will strengthen you and guard you from the evil one.

2 Thessalonians 3:3

PROVISION

The LORD is my shepherd; I have all that I need. He lets me rest in green meadows; he leads me beside peaceful streams. He renews my strength. He guides me along right paths, bringing honor to his name.

Psalm 23:1-3

He gives food to those who fear him; he always remembers his covenant.

Psalm 111:5

Why worry about your clothing? Look at the lilies of the field and how they grow. They don't work or make their clothing, yet Solomon in all his glory was not dressed as beautifully as they are. And if God cares so wonderfully for wildflowers that are here today and thrown into the fire tomorrow, he will certainly care for you.

Matthew 6:28-30

Don't worry about these things, saying, "What will we eat? What will we drink? What will we wear?" These things dominate the thoughts of unbelievers, but your heavenly Father already knows all your needs. Seek the Kingdom of God above all else, and live righteously, and he will give you everything you need.

Matthew 6:31-33

What is the price of five sparrows—two copper coins? Yet God does not forget a single one of them. And the very hairs on your head are all numbered. So don't be afraid; you are more valuable to God than a whole flock of sparrows.

Luke 12:6-7

This same God who takes care of me will supply all your needs from his glorious riches, which have been given to us in Christ Jesus.

Philippians 4:19

PURPOSE

I cry out to God Most High, to God who will fulfill his purpose for me.

Psalm 57:2

Turn my eyes from worthless things, and give me life through your word.

Psalm 119:37

I knew you before I formed you in your mother's womb. Before you were born I set you apart.

Jeremiah 1:5

Don't copy the behavior and customs of this world, but let God transform you into a new person by changing the way you think. Then you will learn to know God's will for you, which is good and pleasing and perfect.

Romans 12:2

I once thought these things were valuable, but now I consider them worthless because of what Christ has done. Yes, everything else is worthless when compared with the infinite value of knowing Christ Jesus my Lord. For his sake I have discarded everything else, counting it all as garbage, so that I could gain Christ and become one with him.

Philippians 3:7-9

I focus on this one thing: Forgetting the past and looking forward to what lies ahead, I press on to reach the end of the race and receive the heavenly prize for which God, through Christ Jesus, is calling us.

Philippians 3:13-14

REPENTANCE

The LORD your God is gracious and merciful. If you return to him, he will not continue to turn his face from you.

2 Chronicles 30:9

The LORD is close to the brokenhearted; he rescues those whose spirits are crushed.

Psalm 34:18

The sacrifice you desire is a broken spirit. You will not reject a broken and repentant heart, O God.

Psalm 51:17

"My wayward children," says the LORD, "come back to me, and I will heal your wayward hearts."

Jeremiah 3:22

If wicked people turn away from all their sins and begin to obey my decrees and do what is just and right, they will surely live and not die.

Ezekiel 18:21

Come back to me and live!

Amos 5:4

Each of you must repent of your sins and turn to God, and be baptized in the name of Jesus Christ for the forgiveness of your sins. Then you will receive the gift of the Holy Spirit.

Acts 2:38

This is a trustworthy saying, and everyone should accept it: "Christ Jesus came into the world to save sinners."

1 Timothy 1:15

SALVATION

The LORD says, "I will rescue those who love me. I will protect those who trust in my name. When they call on me, I will answer; I will be with them in trouble. I will rescue and honor them. I will reward them with a long life and give them my salvation."

Psalm 91:14-16

If wicked people turn away from all their sins and begin to obey my decrees and do what is just and right, they will surely live and not die.

Ezekiel 18:21

Jesus replied, "I tell you the truth, unless you are born again, you cannot see the Kingdom of God."

John 3:3

God loved the world so much that he gave his one and only Son, so that everyone who believes in him will not perish but have eternal life.

John 3:16

Believe in the Lord Jesus and you will be saved.

Acts 16:31

Since our friendship with God was restored by the death of his Son while we were still his enemies, we will certainly be saved through the life of his Son.

Romans 5:10

If you confess with your mouth that Jesus is Lord and believe in your heart that God raised him from the dead, you will be saved.

Romans 10:9

This means that anyone who belongs to Christ has become a new person. The old life is gone; a new life has begun!

2 Corinthians 5:17

Because we are united with Christ, we have received an inheritance from God, for he chose us in advance, and he makes everything work out according to his plan.

Ephesians 1:11

When God our Savior revealed his kindness and love, he saved us, not because of the righteous things we had done, but because of his mercy. He washed away our sins, giving us a new birth and new life through the Holy Spirit. He generously poured out the Spirit upon us through Jesus Christ our Savior.

Titus 3:4-6

Just as each person is destined to die once and after that comes judgment, so also Christ died once for all time as a sacrifice to take away the sins of many people. He will come again, not to deal with our sins, but to bring salvation to all who are eagerly waiting for him.

Hebrews 9:27-28

SICKNESS

—— ⚘ ——

I am the LORD who heals you.

Exodus 15:26

My health may fail, and my spirit may grow weak, but God remains the strength of my heart; he is mine forever.

Psalm 73:26

He forgives all my sins and heals all my diseases.

Psalm 103:3

The LORD will guide you continually, giving you water when you are dry and restoring your strength. You will be like a well-watered garden, like an ever-flowing spring.

Isaiah 58:11

O LORD, if you heal me, I will be truly healed; if you save me, I will be truly saved. My praises are for you alone!

Jeremiah 17:14

"I will give you back your health and heal your wounds," says the LORD.

Jeremiah 30:17

For you who fear my name, the Sun of Righteousness will rise with healing in his wings. And you will go free, leaping with joy like calves let out to pasture.

Malachi 4:2

Do not waste time arguing over godless ideas and old wives' tales. Instead, train yourself to be godly. "Physical training is good, but training for godliness is much better, promising benefits in this life and in the life to come."

1 Timothy 4:7-8

He personally carried our sins in his body on the cross so that we can be dead to sin and live for what is right. By his wounds you are healed.

1 Peter 2:24

I heard a loud shout from the throne, saying, "Look, God's home is now among his people! He will live with them, and they will be his people. God himself will be with them. He will wipe every tear from their eyes, and there will be no more death or sorrow or crying or pain. All these things are gone forever."

Revelation 21:3-4

SIN

Though your sins are like scarlet, I will make them as white as snow. Though they are red like crimson, I will make them as white as wool.

Isaiah 1:18

He was pierced for our rebellion, crushed for our sins. He was beaten so we could be whole. He was whipped so we could be healed. All of us, like sheep, have strayed away. We have left God's paths to follow our own. Yet the LORD laid on him the sins of us all.

Isaiah 53:5-6

We know that our old sinful selves were crucified with Christ so that sin might lose its power in our lives. We are no longer slaves to sin. For when we died with Christ we were set free from the power of sin.

Romans 6:6-7

Sin is no longer your master, for you no longer live under the requirements of the law. Instead, you live under the freedom of God's grace.

Romans 6:14

The wages of sin is death, but the free gift of God is eternal life through Christ Jesus our Lord.

Romans 6:23

Jesus gave his life for our sins, just as God our Father planned, in order to rescue us from this evil world in which we live.

Galatians 1:4

He is so rich in kindness and grace that he purchased our freedom with the blood of his Son and forgave our sins.

Ephesians 1:7

He personally carried our sins in his body on the cross so that we can be dead to sin and live for what is right. By his wounds you are healed.

1 Peter 2:24

If we confess our sins to him, he is faithful and just to forgive us our sins and to cleanse us from all wickedness.

1 John 1:9

If anyone does sin, we have an advocate who pleads our case before the Father. He is Jesus Christ, the one who is truly righteous. He himself is the sacrifice that atones for our sins—and not only our sins but the sins of all the world.

1 John 2:1-2

STARTING OVER

He renews my strength. He guides me along right paths, bringing honor to his name.

Psalm 23:3

Create in me a clean heart, O God. Renew a loyal spirit within me.

Psalm 51:10

Remember your promise to me; it is my only hope. Your promise revives me; it comforts me in all my troubles.

Psalm 119:49-50

Though your sins are like scarlet, I will make them as white as snow. Though they are red like crimson, I will make them as white as wool.

Isaiah 1:18

Great is his faithfulness; his mercies begin afresh each morning.

Lamentations 3:23

I will give you a new heart, and I will put a new spirit in you. I will take out your stony, stubborn heart and give you a tender, responsive heart.

Ezekiel 36:26

We are made right with God by placing our faith in Jesus Christ. And this is true for everyone who believes, no matter who we are.

Romans 3:22

Don't copy the behavior and customs of this world, but let God transform you into a new person by changing the way you think. Then you will learn to know God's will for you, which is good and pleasing and perfect.

Romans 12:2

Anyone who belongs to Christ has become a new person. The old life is gone; a new life has begun!

2 Corinthians 5:17

God, who began the good work within you, will continue his work until it is finally finished on the day when Christ Jesus returns.

Philippians 1:6

The one sitting on the throne said, "Look, I am making everything new!"

Revelation 21:5

STRENGTH

My health may fail, and my spirit may grow weak, but God remains the strength of my heart; he is mine forever.

Psalm 73:26

As soon as I pray, you answer me; you encourage me by giving me strength.

Psalm 138:3

He gives power to the weak and strength to the powerless. Even youths will become weak and tired, and young men will fall in exhaustion. But those who trust in the LORD will find new strength. They will soar high on wings like eagles. They will run and not grow weary. They will walk and not faint.

Isaiah 10:29-31

Don't be afraid, for I am with you. Don't be discouraged, for I am your God. I will strengthen you and help you. I will hold you up with my victorious right hand.

Isaiah 41:10

The Sovereign LORD is my strength! He makes me as surefooted as a deer, able to tread upon the heights.

Habakkuk 3:19

It is not by force nor by strength, but by my Spirit, says the LORD of Heaven's Armies.

Zechariah 4:6

Now all glory to God, who is able, through his mighty power at work within us, to accomplish infinitely more than we might ask or think.

Ephesians 3:20

I can do everything through Christ, who gives me strength.

Philippians 4:13

SUFFERING

The LORD is close to the brokenhearted; he rescues those whose spirits are crushed. The righteous person faces many troubles, but the LORD comes to the rescue each time.

Psalm 34:18-19

Remember your promise to me; it is my only hope. Your promise revives me; it comforts me in all my troubles.

Psalm 119:49-50

The LORD helps the fallen and lifts those bent beneath their loads.

Psalm 145:14

He heals the brokenhearted and bandages their wounds.

Psalm 147:3

Sing for joy, O heavens! Rejoice, O earth! Burst into song, O mountains! For the LORD has comforted his people and will have compassion on them in their suffering.

Isaiah 49:13

In all their suffering he also suffered, and he personally rescued them. In his love and mercy he redeemed them. He lifted them up and carried them through all the years.

Isaiah 63:9

Come back to the place of safety, all you prisoners who still have hope! I promise this very day that I will repay two blessings for each of your troubles.

Zechariah 9:12

All praise to God, the Father of our Lord Jesus Christ. God is our merciful Father and the source of all comfort. He comforts us in all our troubles so that we can comfort others. When they are troubled, we will be able to give them the same comfort God has given us.

2 Corinthians 1:3-4

The more we suffer for Christ, the more God will shower us with his comfort through Christ.

2 Corinthians 1:5

Don't be afraid of what you are about to suffer. The devil will throw some of you into prison to test you. You will suffer for ten days. But if you remain faithful even when facing death, I will give you the crown of life.

Revelation 2:10

The Lamb on the throne will be their Shepherd. He will lead them to springs of life-giving water. And God will wipe every tear from their eyes.

Revelation 7:17

TEMPTATION

—— ∽⊙⊙∾ ——

Oh, the joys of those who do not follow the advice of the wicked, or stand around with sinners, or join in with mockers.

Psalm 1:1

Victory comes from you, O LORD. May you bless your people.

Psalm 3:8

The path of the virtuous leads away from evil; whoever follows that path is safe.

Proverbs 16:17

Temptations are inevitable, but what sorrow awaits the person who does the tempting.

Matthew 18:7

The temptations in your life are no different from what others experience. And God is faithful. He will not allow the temptation to be more than you can stand. When you are tempted, he will show you a way out so that you can endure.

1 Corinthians 10:13

The Lord is faithful; he will strengthen you and guard you from the evil one.

2 Thessalonians 3:3

It was necessary for him to be made in every respect like us, his brothers and sisters, so that he could be our merciful and faithful High Priest before God. Then he could offer a sacrifice that would take away the sins of the people. Since he himself has gone through suffering and testing, he is able to help us when we are being tested.

Hebrews 2:17-18

This High Priest of ours understands our weaknesses, for he faced all of the same testings we do, yet he did not sin.

Hebrews 4:15

Remember, when you are being tempted, do not say, "God is tempting me." God is never tempted to do wrong, and he never tempts anyone else.

James 1:13

Temptation comes from our own desires, which entice us and drag us away. These desires give birth to sinful actions. And when sin is allowed to grow, it gives birth to death.

James 1:14-15

TROUBLED TIMES

The LORD is a shelter for the oppressed, a refuge in times of trouble.

Psalm 9:9

You are my hiding place; you protect me from trouble. You surround me with songs of victory.

Psalm 32:7

The righteous person faces many troubles, but the LORD comes to the rescue each time.

Psalm 34:19

The LORD rescues the godly; he is their fortress in times of trouble.

Psalm 37:39

God is our refuge and strength, always ready to help in times of trouble. So we will not fear when earthquakes come and the mountains crumble into the sea.

Psalm 46:1-2

Call on me when you are in trouble, and I will rescue you, and you will give me glory.

Psalm 50:15

You have allowed me to suffer much hardship, but you will restore me to life again and lift me up from the depths of the earth.

Psalm 71:20

I will call to you whenever I'm in trouble, and you will answer me.

Psalm 86:7

Those who plant in tears will harvest with shouts of joy. They weep as they go to plant their seed, but they sing as they return with the harvest.

Psalm 126:5-6

Though I am surrounded by troubles, you will protect me from the anger of my enemies. You reach out your hand, and the power of your right hand saves me.

Psalm 138:7

LORD, be merciful to us, for we have waited for you. Be our strong arm each day and our salvation in times of trouble.

Isaiah 33:2

No one is abandoned by the Lord forever. Though he brings grief, he also shows compassion because of the greatness of his unfailing love. For he does not enjoy hurting people or causing them sorrow.

Lamentations 3:31-33

The LORD is good, a strong refuge when trouble comes. He is close to those who trust in him.

Nahum 1:7

I have told you all this so that you may have peace in me. Here on earth you will have many trials and sorrows. But take heart, because I have overcome the world.

John 16:33

Our present troubles are small and won't last very long. Yet they produce for us a glory that vastly outweighs them and will last forever!

2 Corinthians 4:17

We don't look at the troubles we can see now; rather, we fix our gaze on things that cannot be seen. For the things we see now will soon be gone, but the things we cannot see will last forever.

2 Corinthians 4:18

TRUSTING GOD

—— ∿⊙☙ ——

God is not a man, so he does not lie. He is not human, so he does not change his mind. Has he ever spoken and failed to act? Has he ever promised and not carried it through?

Numbers 23:19

Trust in the LORD and do good. Then you will live safely in the land and prosper. Take delight in the LORD, and he will give you your heart's desires. Commit everything you do to the LORD. Trust him, and he will help you.

Psalm 37:3-5

God is our refuge and strength, always ready to help in times of trouble. So we will not fear when earthquakes come and the mountains crumble into the sea.

Psalm 46:1-2

That is what God is like. He is our God forever and ever, and he will guide us until we die.

Psalm 48:14

O LORD of Heaven's Armies, what joy for those who trust in you.

Psalm 84:12

The LORD keeps watch over you as you come and go, both now and forever.

Psalm 121:8

Trust in the LORD with all your heart; do not depend on your own understanding. Seek his will in all you do, and he will show you which path to take.

Proverbs 3:5-6

You will keep in perfect peace all who trust in you, all whose thoughts are fixed on you!

Isaiah 26:3

The grass withers and the flowers fade, but the word of our God stands forever.

Isaiah 40:8

Blessed are those who trust in the LORD and have made the LORD their hope and confidence. They are like trees planted along a riverbank, with roots that reach deep into the water. Such trees are not bothered by the heat or worried by long months of drought. Their leaves stay green, and they never stop producing fruit.

Jeremiah 17:7-8

LORD, you remain the same forever! Your throne continues from generation to generation.

Lamentations 5:19

I am the LORD, and I do not change.

Malachi 3:6

God will do this, for he is faithful to do what he says, and he has invited you into partnership with his Son, Jesus Christ our Lord.

1 Corinthians 1:9

If we are faithful to the end, trusting God just as firmly as when we first believed, we will share in all that belongs to Christ.

Hebrews 3:14

Let us hold tightly without wavering to the hope we affirm, for God can be trusted to keep his promise.

Hebrews 10:23

Jesus Christ is the same yesterday, today, and forever.

Hebrews 13:8

Give all your worries and cares to God, for he cares about you.

1 Peter 5:7

WEARINESS

He renews my strength. He guides me along right paths, bringing honor to his name.

Psalm 23:3

My health may fail, and my spirit may grow weak, but God remains the strength of my heart; he is mine forever.

Psalm 73:26

He fills my life with good things. My youth is renewed like the eagle's!

Psalm 103:5

God gives rest to his loved ones.

Psalm 127:2

Those who refresh others will themselves be refreshed.

Proverbs 11:25

He gives power to the weak and strength to the powerless. Even youths will become weak and tired, and young men will fall in exhaustion. But those who trust in the LORD will find new strength. They will soar high on wings like eagles. They will run and not grow weary. They will walk and not faint.

Isaiah 40:29-31

I have given rest to the weary and joy to the sorrowing.

Jeremiah 31:25

Come to me, all of you who are weary and carry heavy burdens, and I will give you rest. Take my yoke upon you. Let me teach you, because I am humble and gentle at heart, and you will find rest for your souls.

Matthew 11:28-29

WILL OF GOD

I cry out to God Most High, to God who will fulfill his purpose for me.

Psalm 57:2

Seek his will in all you do, and he will show you which path to take.

Proverbs 3:6

We can make our plans, but the LORD determines our steps.

Proverbs 16:9

The LORD of Heaven's Armies has spoken—who can change his plans? When his hand is raised, who can stop him?

Isaiah 14:27

"I know the plans I have for you," says the LORD. "They are plans for good and not for disaster, to give you a future and a hope."

Jeremiah 29:11

Anyone who does the will of my Father in heaven is my brother and sister and mother!

Matthew 12:50

Don't copy the behavior and customs of this world, but let God transform you into a new person by changing the way you think. Then you will learn to know God's will for you, which is good and pleasing and perfect.

Romans 12:2

Because we are united with Christ, we have received an inheritance from God, for he chose us in advance, and he makes everything work out according to his plan.

Ephesians 1:11

If you need wisdom, ask our generous God, and he will give it to you. He will not rebuke you for asking. But when you ask him, be sure that your faith is in God alone. Do not waver, for a person with divided loyalty is as unsettled as a wave of the sea that is blown and tossed by the wind.

James 1:5-6

We are confident that he hears us whenever we ask for anything that pleases him.

1 John 5:14

WISDOM

I will bless the LORD who guides me; even at night my heart instructs me.

Psalm 16:7

Fear of the LORD is the foundation of true wisdom. All who obey his commandments will grow in wisdom.

Psalm 111:10

You will understand what it means to fear the LORD, and you will gain knowledge of God. For the LORD grants wisdom! From his mouth come knowledge and understanding. He grants a treasure of common sense to the honest. He is a shield to those who walk with integrity.

Proverbs 2:5-7

Trust in the LORD with all your heart; do not depend on your own understanding. Seek his will in all you do, and he will show you which path to take.

Proverbs 3:5-6

Joyful is the person who finds wisdom, the one who gains understanding.

Proverbs 3:13

The wise inherit honor, but fools are put to shame!

Proverbs 3:35

Fear of the LORD is the foundation of wisdom. Knowledge of the Holy One results in good judgment.

Proverbs 9:10

To acquire wisdom is to love oneself; people who cherish understanding will prosper.

Proverbs 19:8

No human wisdom or understanding or plan can stand against the LORD.

Proverbs 21:30

The wise are mightier than the strong, and those with knowledge grow stronger and stronger.

Proverbs 24:5

God gives wisdom, knowledge, and joy to those who please him.

Ecclesiastes 2:26

He will teach us his ways, and we will walk in his paths.

Isaiah 2:3

God, who said, "Let there be light in the darkness," has made this light shine in our hearts so we could know the glory of God that is seen in the face of Jesus Christ.

2 Corinthians 4:6

If you need wisdom, ask our generous God, and he will give it to you. He will not rebuke you for asking.

James 1:5

WORD OF GOD

——— ❧ ❧ ———

Study this Book of Instruction continually. Meditate on it day and night so you will be sure to obey everything written in it. Only then will you prosper and succeed in all you do.

Joshua 1:8

The laws of the LORD are true; each one is fair. They are more desirable than gold, even the finest gold. They are sweeter than honey, even honey dripping from the comb. They are a warning to your servant, a great reward for those who obey them.

Psalm 19:9-11

Open my eyes to see the wonderful truths in your instructions.

Psalm 119:18

Your laws please me; they give me wise advice.

Psalm 119:24

I meditate on your age-old regulations; O LORD, they comfort me.

Psalm 119:52

Your word is a lamp to guide my feet and a light for my path.

Psalm 119:105

The teaching of your word gives light, so even the simple can understand.

Psalm 119:130

The grass withers and the flowers fade, but the word of our God stands forever.

Isaiah 40:8

The rain and snow come down from the heavens and stay on the ground to water the earth. They cause the grain to grow, producing seed for the farmer and bread for the hungry. It is the same with my word. I send it out, and it always produces fruit. It will accomplish all I want it to, and it will prosper everywhere I send it.

Isaiah 55:10-11

Heaven and earth will disappear, but my words will never disappear.

Matthew 24:35

Jesus replied, "But even more blessed are all who hear the word of God and put it into practice."

Luke 11:28

Such things were written in the Scriptures long ago to teach us. And the Scriptures give us hope and encouragement as we wait patiently for God's promises to be fulfilled.

Romans 15:4

All Scripture is inspired by God and is useful to teach us what is true and to make us realize what is wrong in our lives. It corrects us when we are wrong and teaches us to do what is right. God uses it to prepare and equip his people to do every good work.

2 Timothy 3:16-17

The word of God is alive and powerful. It is sharper than the sharpest two-edged sword, cutting between soul and spirit, between joint and marrow. It exposes our innermost thoughts and desires.

Hebrews 4:12

I will put my laws in their minds, and I will write them on their hearts. I will be their God, and they will be my people.

Hebrews 8:10

Get rid of all the filth and evil in your lives, and humbly accept the word God has planted in your hearts, for it has the power to save your souls.

James 1:21

If you look carefully into the perfect law that sets you free, and if you do what it says and don't forget what you heard, then God will bless you for doing it.

James 1:25

You have been born again, but not to a life that will quickly end. Your new life will last forever because it comes from the eternal, living word of God. As the Scriptures say, "People are like grass; their beauty is like a flower in the field. The grass withers and the flower fades. But the word of the Lord remains forever." And that word is the Good News that was preached to you.

1 Peter 1:23-25

WORK

As for you, be strong and courageous, for your work will be rewarded.

2 Chronicles 15:7

Unless the LORD builds a house, the work of the builders is wasted.

Psalm 127:1

On the judgment day, fire will reveal what kind of work each builder has done. The fire will show if a person's work has any value. If the work survives, that builder will receive a reward. But if the work is burned up, the builder will suffer great loss. The builder will be saved, but like someone barely escaping through a wall of flames.

1 Corinthians 3:13-15

My dear brothers and sisters, be strong and immovable. Always work enthusiastically for the Lord, for you know that nothing you do for the Lord is ever useless.

1 Corinthians 15:58

Remember this—a farmer who plants only a few seeds will get a small crop. But the one who plants generously will get a generous crop.

2 Corinthians 9:6

Pay careful attention to your own work, for then you will get the satisfaction of a job well done, and you won't need to compare yourself to anyone else. For we are each responsible for our own conduct.

Galatians 6:4-5

He makes the whole body fit together perfectly. As each part does its own special work, it helps the other parts grow, so that the whole body is healthy and growing and full of love.

Ephesians 4:16

Work with enthusiasm, as though you were working for the Lord rather than for people. Remember that the Lord will reward each one of us for the good we do.

Ephesians 6:7-8

Work willingly at whatever you do, as though you were working for the Lord rather than for people. Remember that the Lord will give you an inheritance as your reward, and that the Master you are serving is Christ.

Colossians 3:23-24

Make it your goal to live a quiet life, minding your own business and working with your hands, just as we instructed you before. Then people who are not Christians will respect the way you live, and you will not need to depend on others.

1 Thessalonians 4:11-12

There is a special rest still waiting for the people of God. For all who have entered into God's rest have rested from their labors, just as God did after creating the world.

Hebrews 4:9-10

God is not unjust. He will not forget how hard you have worked for him and how you have shown your love to him by caring for other believers, as you still do.

Hebrews 6:10

WORSHIP

Let all who take refuge in you rejoice; let them sing joyful praises forever. Spread your protection over them, that all who love your name may be filled with joy.

Psalm 5:11

Praise the LORD, for he has shown me the wonders of his unfailing love. He kept me safe when my city was under attack.

Psalm 31:21

It is good to give thanks to the LORD, to sing praises to the Most High.

Psalm 92:1

Come, let us worship and bow down. Let us kneel before the LORD our maker, for he is our God. We are the people he watches over, the flock under his care.

Psalm 95:6-7

When he comes on that day, he will receive glory from his holy people—praise from all who believe. And this includes you, for you believed what we told you about him.

2 Thessalonians 1:10

You are worthy, O Lord our God, to receive glory and honor and power. For you created all things, and they exist because you created what you pleased.

Revelation 4:11

Who will not fear you, Lord, and glorify your name? For you alone are holy. All nations will come and worship before you, for your righteous deeds have been revealed.

Revelation 15:4